You Are There!

March on
Washington

August 28, 1963

Torrey Maloof

Consultants

Timothy Rasinski, Ph.D.
Kent State University

Lori Oczkus, M.A.
Literacy Consultant

Publishing Credits

Rachelle Cracchiolo, M.S.Ed., *Publisher*
Conni Medina, M.A.Ed., *Managing Editor*
Dona Herweck Rice, *Series Developer*
Emily R. Smith, M.A.Ed., *Content Director*
Stephanie Bernard/Noelle Cristea, M.A.Ed., *Editors*
Robin Erickson, *Senior Graphic Designer*

The TIME logo is a registered trademark of TIME Inc. Used under license.

Image Credits: Cover and pp. 1, 18-19, 21 Bettmann/Getty Images; p. 4 NBC/NBCU Photo Bank via Getty Images; pp. 4-5 Granger, NYC; p. 6 Hulton Archive/Getty Images; p. 8 Everett Collection Inc/Alamy Stock Photo; p. 9 Paul Slade/Paris Match via Getty Images; p. 11 Paul Slade/Paris Match via Getty Images; p. 12 Everett Collection Inc/Alamy Stock Photo; p. 14 PhotoQuest/Getty Images; p. 15 Everett Collection Inc/Alamy Stock Photo; pp. 16-17 AFP/AFP/Getty Images; p. 20 Everett Collection Inc/Alamy Stock Photo; p. 22 vintageusa1/Alamy Stock Photo; p. 24 Lyndon B. Johnson Library photo by Yoichi Okamoto; p. 25 Everett Collection Inc/Alamy Stock Photo; all other images from iStock and/or Shutterstock

Library of Congress Cataloging-in-Publication Data

Names: Maloof, Torrey, author.
Title: You are there! March on Washington, August 28, 1963 / Torrey Maloof.
Description: Huntington Beach, CA : Teacher Created Materials, [2017] |
  Includes index. | Audience: Grades 7-8.
Identifiers: LCCN 2016052269 (print) | LCCN 2016052831 (ebook) | ISBN
  9781493839292 (pbk.) | ISBN 9781480757899 (eBook)
Subjects: LCSH: March on Washington for Jobs and Freedom (1963 : Washington,
  D.C.)--Juvenile literature. | King, Martin Luther, Jr., 1929-1968. I have
  a dream--Juvenile literature. | Civil rights demonstrations--Washington
  (D.C.)--History--20th century--Juvenile literature. | African
  Americans--Civil rights--History--20th century--Juvenile literature.
Classification: LCC F200 .M335 2017 (print) | LCC F200 (ebook) | DDC
  323.1196/0730904--dc23
LC record available at https://lccn.loc.gov/2016052269

Teacher Created Materials

5301 Oceanus Drive
Huntington Beach, CA 92649-1030
http://www.tcmpub.com

ISBN 978-1-4938-3929-2
© 2017 Teacher Created Materials, Inc.
Printed in China
Nordica.022018.CA21701403

Table of Contents

A DREAM
THER KING, JR.
ON WASHINGTON
AND FREEDOM
T 28, 1963

"They're Pouring In From All Over"

Typically, the city streets are quiet in the early morning hours in Washington, DC, but that is not the case today. Buses are **inundating** the city at a feverish pace, and the smell of diesel exhaust is thick in the air as bus after bus heads to the heart of the nation's capital.

Some are local city buses transporting the residents of DC. Other buses are from bordering states such as Virginia or Maryland. And then there are those passengers that have traveled many miles to reach this destination. There are buses from Massachusetts, Alabama, Michigan, and other states. These buses are carrying eager and committed citizens who want to do their part to make a difference. They don't want to witness history. They want to change history, and today they will.

The March

On August 28, 1963, the March on Washington for Jobs and Freedom took place in the nation's capital. The intent was to bring national attention to the inequality and **racism** African Americans in the United States faced.

While the many buses jam the asphalt arteries of the capital, pedestrians begin to fill the sidewalks on this cool, calm morning. Many of the people are dressed in their Sunday best, wearing suits and dresses. Other people wear hats and sunglasses, and many are carrying sack lunches.

African Americans aren't the only ones walking; there are white people, too. There are elderly people in wheelchairs and young children being pushed in strollers. People of all ages, ethnicities, and **creeds** have come together for this one extraordinary event.

AMERICA!
Why Not
NOW?

Who Could March?

Organizers of the march called for "all Americans of good will who will subscribe to the aims and purposes of the March" to join them to "demand an end to the twin evils of racism and economic **degradation**."

A sense of unity and excitement fills the air with each passing step. Polite conversations mix with the sound of shuffling feet on the cool pavement and the noisy chugging of the buses in the crowded streets. The **colossal** crowd is making its way toward the towering **obelisk** of the Washington Monument.

Sack Lunches

Organizers of the march encouraged attendees to bring their own sack lunches. They suggested a peanut butter and jelly sandwich, fruit, plain cake, and a soft drink. They urged marchers to avoid foods that could spoil in the day's heat, such as mayonnaise and salads.

Meeting at the Monument

Nearing the Washington Monument, it becomes virtually impossible to maneuver through the **throng** of people. The pressing crowd is growing larger with each passing minute. It is nearing 10 a.m., and the temperature of the air is starting to rise rapidly. People are using event programs and hand fans to keep cool.

The **congregation** at the monument is packed but peaceful. As more marchers arrive, they proceed to check-in stations. There are 40,000 people already present. Organizers want to make sure that each person at the march is accounted for and kept safe.

Premade picket signs with writing demanding equal rights, decent housing, and more jobs are handed out among the crowd. Marchers can be seen proudly hoisting them in the air as if they are practicing for the main event. Amid the clamor, the testing of a microphone, "Testing, one, two, testing," can be heard over loudspeakers.

Approved Signs Only

The only signs allowed at the march were ones that the organizers had printed prior to the day's events. They were white signs with red or blue lettering. Some of the slogans included:

We Demand Voting Rights Now!
Civil Rights Plus Full Employment Equals Freedom
Gradually Isn't Fast Enough!

Raising Funds

Many of the participants sported buttons showing a black hand and a white hand shaking, the day's date, and the name of the march. These buttons were sold months in advance to raise funds for the march.

MARCH ON WASHINGTON FOR JOBS & FREEDOM AUGUST 28, 1963

Prior to the official march from the Washington Monument to the Lincoln Memorial, various folk singers and famous personalities excite and inspire the ever-growing crowd. Josephine Baker, a celebrated African American entertainer, is in attendance. She has flown all the way from France to address the protesters. Baker strongly opposes **segregation** and racism. She devotes much of her time to making the world a better and safer place to live. She wholeheartedly gives her support to the American civil rights movement.

Wearing her French military uniform from her time serving in the French Resistance during World War II, Baker speaks with **conviction**; her voice booms through the loudspeaker:

> *I have walked into the palaces of kings and queens and into the houses of presidents. And much more. But I could not walk into a hotel in America and get a cup of coffee, and that made me mad. And when I get mad, you know that I open my big mouth. And then look out, 'cause when Josephine opens her mouth, they hear it all over the world.*

Boisterous Baker

Josephine Baker was born in America but became a star in France. She earned her fame and fortune as a singer, dancer, and actress. She was known to be outspoken and **eccentric**. She even had a pet leopard that she would take for walks on the streets of Paris.

Scratch the Skit

Hollywood celebrities such as Harry Belafonte, Sidney Poitier, Paul Newman, and Marlon Brando were flying in to show their support. They were to perform a skit to entertain the crowd before the march began; however, their flights from the West Coast were late, and the skit was scratched.

Singing for Change

Soon, another woman's voice is heard over the loudspeaker singing the old **ballad** "Oh Freedom." It is the famous folk singer Joan Baez (shown above). Before long, the crowd joins her, "And before I'll be a slave, I'll be buried in my grave / And go home to my Lord and be free / Oh freedom / Oh freedom." The sound of everyone singing in harmony creates a beautiful and breathtaking moment of **solidarity**.

Tribute Song

American folk singer Bob Dylan (shown below) performed his song "Only a Pawn in Their Game" at the march. The song is about Medgar Evers, the civil rights activist who was shot to death by a white **supremacist** in June 1963.

The folk group Peter, Paul, and Mary also steps onto the makeshift stage and performs songs for the crowd. As they sing Bob Dylan's song "Blowin' in the Wind," the heavy weight of the words brings a **solemn** tone to the occasion, further reminding the crowd why they have gathered here today. "How many deaths will it take till he knows / that too many people have died? / The answer, my friend, is blowin' in the wind." Other powerful and touching songs are performed, creating a churchlike atmosphere in the shadow of the Washington Monument.

We Cannot Turn Back

The crowd continues to grow, and people are now packed like **sardines** in a tin can. Jackie Robinson, legendary American baseball player, walks to the podium. Standing in a suit and tie, he proudly proclaims, "I know all of us are going to go away feeling we cannot turn back." Change is on the horizon and everyone can feel it. The crowd starts to grow restless and is eager to begin the march to the Lincoln Memorial.

An announcement is made stating that 90,000 people have arrived, and there are still more coming. Demonstrators roar with excitement, and the atmosphere becomes electric.

STOP! THINK...

This is a picture of legendary baseball player Jackie Robinson and his son, David, at the march.

◉ Why would Robinson bring his son to the March on Washington?

◉ How do you think Robinson's attendance impacted the march?

Time to March

The trek to the Lincoln Memorial is scheduled to begin at 11:30 a.m. and covers almost two miles. However, the restless group needs no prompting. They begin to head toward the Lincoln Memorial early. The massive crowd splits, some marchers walking on Constitution Avenue and some walking on Independence Avenue. They **reconverge** at the statue of Lincoln.

Long, thick cables stretch the length of the route, carrying television and radio signals. Reporters vividly describe the scene to the millions of people listening and watching from their homes. The protesters proudly march for all the world to see—singing, chanting, and waving their signs.

Where Are the Leaders?

The leaders and organizers of the march, including Dr. Martin Luther King Jr., were supposed to lead the people in the march to the Lincoln Memorial. However, they were running late. They were busy meeting with Congress to discuss the passing of the civil rights bill. When word reached them that the people had begun to march, they were quickly escorted to the front of the marchers.

Heat Exhaustion

Along the way, the heat created from the mixture of sun, asphalt, and the **populous** environment caused some people to pass out from heat exhaustion. They were treated at first aid stations along the route.

As they march, some groups sing **hymns** while others chant, "Freedom! Freedom!" Sometimes the weight of the moment causes people to pause and reflect silently. During these moments, all that can be heard is the sound of hundreds of thousands of feet shuffling down the asphalt toward change.

It is nearly 2 p.m., and a quarter of a million people have gathered at the National Mall in front of the Lincoln Memorial. The main program is about to begin. Opera singer Camilla Williams takes the stage at the top of the marble stairs under Lincoln's watchful stone eyes and performs the national anthem. Her patriotic rendition of "The Star-Spangled Banner" is followed by an **invocation** by the Catholic **archbishop** of Washington.

The Star-Spangled Banner

In September 1814, Francis Scott Key wrote the poem "The Defense of Fort McHenry" about his experience during the War of 1812. He described the British bombard Fort McHenry in Maryland. Key described the event as an apparent victory for the British. "It seemed as though mother earth had opened and was vomiting shot and shell in a sheet of fire and brimstone," he would later share. He described how the sight of the U.S. flag still proudly waving over Fort McHenry at dawn became the inspiration for the poem. It was later set to music, **morphing** into America's national anthem, "The Star-Spangled Banner."

The Lincoln Connection

One hundred years earlier, President Abraham Lincoln gave a very famous speech that came to be known as the Gettysburg Address. His speech, invoking the Declaration of Independence, spoke about equality and freedom. "Fourscore and seven years ago our fathers brought forth, on this continent, a new nation, conceived in liberty, and dedicated to the proposition that all men are created equal." It was no coincidence that the organizers of the march chose to deliver their speeches at the Lincoln Memorial.

Next, the director of the march, A. Philip Randolph, walks to the podium and proclaims, "We're gathered here for the longest demonstration in the history of this nation. Let the nation and the world know the meaning of our numbers." His words are met with thunderous applause and cheers from the crowd.

Numerous civil rights leaders and activists take to the stage and **orate** on the importance of the fight for civil rights and equality. They speak with strength and conviction, and their poise and demeanors are calm but mighty. Their carefully chosen words motivate and inspire those in attendance. The words "amen" and "yes" are uttered throughout the crowd.

Later that afternoon, Randolph returns to the stage and introduces the next speaker as the "moral leader of our nation." The crowd erupts in a **frenzy**, applauding and cheering for what seems like an eternity. The oppressive heat and long day don't subdue the excitement; *this* is the moment everyone has been waiting for.

John Lewis

John Lewis was the youngest speaker of the day. He was 23 years old. Organizers were worried that his speech would be too lively and controversial. Lewis was eager for change and did not want to wait patiently for the government to get behind the civil rights movement. However, he was persuaded to tone down the content of his speech. Lewis agreed, but his fiery, passionate words still evoked the type of response from the crowd he was looking for.

Speaking for Change

To the side of the stage stands Dr. Martin Luther King Jr. Before he takes the podium, African American vocalist Mahalia Jackson sings. Her commanding voice carries an old slave **spiritual** to the masses. "I been 'buked and I been scorned / I'm gonna tell my Lord / When I get home / Just how long you've been treating me wrong." Jackson's song **invigorates** the crowd. The wild cheering and chanting slowly die down as King begins to speak into the microphone.

At first when King speaks, he reads his words from a paper, but before long he discards his prepared words and speaks from his heart. His **cadence** grabs the crowd's full attention. He speaks for 17 minutes as he delivers his "I Have a Dream" speech.

Marian Anderson Sings

Marian Anderson, one of the most celebrated African American singers of the day, was scheduled to perform the national anthem at the start of the march. However, she was delayed in arriving, so she instead sang "He's Got the Whole World in His Hands" after King concluded his speech.

King's powerful words will never be forgotten:

*When we allow freedom to ring—
when we let it ring from every city
and every **hamlet**, from every
state and every city, we will
be able to speed up that
day when all of God's
children, black men and
white men, Jews and
Gentiles, Protestants
and Catholics, will be
able to join hands and
sing in the words of
the old Negro spiritual,
"Free at last, Free at
last, Great God a-mighty,
We are free at last."*

THINK LINK

◎ Why do you think King was the last speaker of the day?

◎ When King says, "free at last," what is he referring to? What will they be freed from?

◎ What did King envision for the future of America?

The Meeting After the March

After the march concluded, its leaders and organizers met with President John F. Kennedy that very same evening. Here are some interesting facts about that meeting:

Location: Oval Office at the White House

Attendees: Mathew Ahmann, Dr. Martin Luther King Jr., John Lewis, Rabbi Joachim Prinz, Reverend Eugene Carson Blake, Walter Ruether, A. Philip Randolph, Whitney M. Young Jr., Floyd McKissick, Secretary of Labor Willard Wirtz, Vice President Lyndon B. Johnson, and President John F. Kennedy

Purpose: to discuss racial inequality and finally pass a civil rights bill that had been in the works for some time

Quote of the Day: As President Kennedy greeted Dr. King, the president smiled and said, "I have a dream." It was his way of giving King **accolades** for his spectacular speech.

Food Served: ham, cheese, and turkey sandwiches with cherry cobbler for dessert

At the march: The civil rights bill that the men discussed in the meeting had been referenced at the march. When Randolph's speech concluded, the crowd chanted, "Pass the bill! Pass the bill!" They hoped to get the attention and support of the 100 members of Congress sitting at the foot of the Lincoln Memorial.

Outcome: The meeting was cordial and successful by all accounts. However, the bill would be stalled and delayed in congressional committees. It would not be signed into law until July 1964.

Reflection

It takes several hours for the **hordes** of people to **dissipate** and the hundreds of buses to leave the city's center. As the sun slowly sets in the western sky, hundreds of people still dot the landscape of the National Mall. Litter and discarded picket signs are strewn across the grounds. Television cameras and journalists remain on the scene, reporting to the nation the day's historic events.

The outside temperature has cooled but a new, fierce fire burns in the hearts of many. The persuasive and powerful speeches given by the movement's greatest civil rights leaders have inspired and energized a nation to take action. Washington and the world at large will never be the same. The air is thick with hopes and dreams, and change is firmly planted on the horizon. The March on Washington for Jobs and Freedom has come to a triumphant culmination.

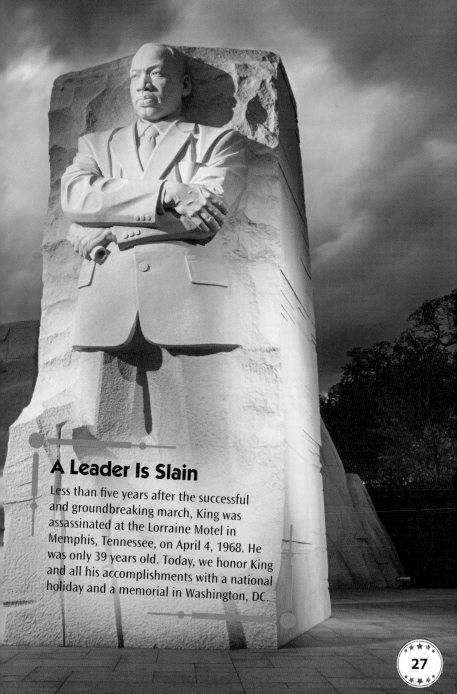

A Leader Is Slain

Less than five years after the successful and groundbreaking march, King was assassinated at the Lorraine Motel in Memphis, Tennessee, on April 4, 1968. He was only 39 years old. Today, we honor King and all his accomplishments with a national holiday and a memorial in Washington, DC.

Glossary

accolades—praise

archbishop—the highest-ranking bishop, an official who ranks higher than a priest, in a particular area

ballad—a popular song that is usually slow and simple

cadence—the rhythmic pattern of a person's voice

colossal—of great size; enormous

congregation—group of people attending a service, often a religious one

conviction—the feeling of being certain in your beliefs

creeds—ideas or beliefs that guide the actions of a group

degradation—decline to a worse or weaker state

dissipate—to spread out and disappear

eccentric—strange; odd

frenzy—a wild or disorderly activity

Gentiles—non-Jewish people

hamlet—a small town

hordes—large groups

hymns—religious songs of praise

inundating— overwhelming

invigorates—gives energy to

invocation—a blessing or prayer given at the beginning of a ceremony or event

morphing—transforming from one thing to another

obelisk—a tall, four-sided pillar that becomes narrow at the top, ending in a point

orate—speak in a formal and serious way

populous—having a large number of people in an area

racism—a belief that one race is superior to other races

reconverge—come back together

sardines—very small fish that often come packed in a can

segregation—the practice or policy of keeping people of different races or religions separate

solemn—very serious or formal in tone or behavior

solidarity—a feeling of unity among a group of people

spiritual—a religious folk song sung by African Americans

supremacist—a person who believes that one group of people is better than all other groups and should have control

throng—a large crowd

Index

Check It Out!

Books

Euchner, Charles. 2010. *Nobody Turn Me Around: A People's History of the 1963 March on Washington.* Beacon Press.

Freed, Leonard. 2013. *This Is the Day: The March on Washington.* Paul Getty Trust.

Jones, William P. 2013. *The March on Washington: Jobs, Freedom, and the Forgotten History of Civil Rights.* W.W. Norton & Company.

Wexler, Sanford. 1993. *The Civil Rights Movement: An Eyewitness History.* Facts on File.

Wiles, Deborah. 2014. *Revolution.* Scholastic Press.

Video

Akomfrah, John. *The March.* PBS.

Websites

History.com. *March on Washington.* http://www.history.com/topics/black-history/march-on-washington.

The Martin Luther King, Jr. Center for Nonviolent Social Change. *The King Center.* http://www.thekingcenter.org/.

Try It!

Imagine you are giving the keynote speech at a rally on an issue that you can not remain silent about. You are also in charge of coming up with five slogans for posters that will be passed out at the rally. Before getting to work, you have some planning to do:

- Make a list of causes that you feel passionate about. Do you feel strongly about a global crisis? Are there national issues you want to speak for or against? Do you want to change something that is happening in your town?

- Look over your list, and select what you feel is the most important issue to spread awareness about.

- Create a list of why people support this cause and what you could say to sway people to rally behind the issue.

- Use this list to come up with five witty slogans for the posters. If you need assistance, research other successful, peaceful protests and use them as inspiration.

- Now it is time to write your speech. It needs to be three minutes long, which means you have a short time to convey your message, inspire the audience, and get your point across. Make sure your message is clear.

- Have a friend look over your speech to suggest edits.

- Read your speech aloud, practicing for timing, tone, and presentation. (If your speech is less than three minutes, slow down around important lines. If your speech is too long, consider cutting some sentences out.)

- Present your speech to your class.

About the Author

Torrey Maloof loves researching and writing books about history's most interesting people and events. She can often be found reading in the sun on the sandy shores of Southern California. Maloof also loves chasing after her niece, Cordelia, who, like her aunt, loves the beach. The two also hold a special place in their hearts for Disneyland and frequently visit the magical theme park together.

IN THIS TEMPLE
AS IN THE HEARTS OF THE PEOPLE
FOR WHOM HE SAVED THE UNION
THE MEMORY OF ABRAHAM LINCOLN
IS ENSHRINED FOREVER